CU00496708

The Traveler's Guide To

Adelaide,
South Australia

*The Insider's Guide to Adelaide:
Get Ready to Be Amazed!*

Helen T. Gaskill

COPYRIGHT NOTICE

DISCLAIMER

TABLE OF CONTENT

Introduction

WELCOME TO ADELAIDE

Adelaide captured my heart the instant I stepped foot in this dynamic city. Welcome to a city that is so much more than that; it is a way of life, a cultural marvel, and a South Australian hidden gem. Allow me to walk you through the details that make Adelaide such a unique location.

Adelaide welcomes you with wide arms and a warm atmosphere. It's a city that exudes warmth and charm, where every street corner tells a tale and each district has its own distinct personality. The calm pace of life and kindness of its inhabitants greet you from the moment you arrive.

Overview of Adelaide's Attractions

What makes Adelaide such a magical destination? It's a synthesis of diverse aspects that work well together. The city is well-known for its festivals, which celebrate culture, the arts, and music throughout the year. The wonderful cuisine, influenced by several cultures, is a culinary voyage in and of itself. Nature intertwines with the urban surroundings, providing a tranquil respite within the city limits.

What to Expect during Your Visit

Be prepared for the unexpected! Adelaide is a city that never ceases to amaze. Its variety has something for everyone. Adelaide caters to your desires whether you are a culture aficionado, a foodie, a nature lover, or an adventure seeker. The city easily flows from lively cityscapes to calm natural getaways, catering to every traveler's diverse tastes.

Adelaide's Historical Background

Adelaide's historical tapestry is rich and captivating. Adelaide, founded in 1836, is a young city with a fascinating history. Its origins as a free settlement have an impact on its distinct personality today. Exploring its past exposes a tale of European colonization, indigenous heritage, and the development of a multicultural culture.

Recognizing the Local Culture

Adelaide's cultural variety is a mash-up of traditions, art, and way of life. Locals are proud of their heritage, which they celebrate through festivals, art galleries, and gastronomic experiences. Understanding the local culture entails immersing oneself in a world where tradition and modernity coexist, where heritage is conserved while embracing the future.

This city is a mash-up of old and new, traditional and modern, presenting a kaleidoscope of experiences that characterize Adelaide's allure. From its historic streets to its current cultural scene, this city captivates visitors from all walks of life.

Chapter 1

GETTING STARTED IN ADELAIDE

Let's get your voyage underway, covering everything from packing essentials to navigating local customs. This is your basic kit for welcoming Adelaide with open arms.

Travel Essentials in Adelaide

Pack for adaptability when visiting Adelaide. The weather here is notorious for changing its mind. Think layers, a strong pair of walking shoes, and don't forget your sunscreen, especially during the warmer months.

Climate and Weather

Adelaide's weather is a story in and of itself. Summers can be sweltering, while winters can be chilly. The best of both worlds can be found in spring and autumn. What is the key? Whatever the season, be ready for everything.

Currency, language, and time zone

Your currency is the Australian dollar. English is spoken, but with a few Aussie slang terms tossed in for good measure! Time? For the most part, that's Australian Central Standard Time (ACST), but it alternates with Daylight Saving Time (ACDT) from October to April.

Considerations for Safety and Health

Adelaide is a relatively safe city; however basic precautions are always prudent. Although the tap water is safe to drink and the medical facilities are excellent, travel insurance is required. Be sun-aware as well; those rays might be deceptive.

Requirements for Entry and Travel Documents

Before you arrive in Adelaide, ensure sure your passport is still valid and that you have a visa if necessary. Remember to preserve a digital or print copy of your itinerary and critical contacts as a backup.

This beginning guide will get you off to a good start in Adelaide. Prepare to be immersed in a city that is both relaxed and energetic, where the sun shines brightly and the people are as warm as the weather.

Chapter 2

EXPLORING ADELAIDE'S HERITAGE

Adelaide's heritage is a lovely mix of history, culture, and architectural marvels that give a vivid picture of the city's illustrious past. Let's get in the time machine and discover the treasures that make Adelaide's heritage so fascinating.

Historic Locations and Landmarks

Adelaide does not disappoint when it comes to history. The city's historic districts, such as Adelaide Oval and Government House, retell stories from bygone ages. Adelaide Town Hall and the Old Gum Tree are examples of the city's history.

Museums and Cultural Institutions

Culture vultures, rejoice! Adelaide is a museum lover's paradise. The South Australian Museum, which houses intriguing displays on natural history and Aboriginal heritage, is a must-see. The Art Gallery of South Australia's remarkable collection of local and international treasures will delight art lovers.

Indigenous legacy Spots

Learn about the indigenous legacy that runs throughout the city. Tandanya National Aboriginal Cultural Institutes, for example, are wonderful venues for disseminating indigenous art, storytelling, and cultural practices. The Kaurna people's connection to this land is visible in different locations throughout Adelaide.

Architectural Wonders

Adelaide's skyline is a work of architectural beauty. The city boasts a remarkable mix of architectural styles, ranging from classic Victorian-era structures like Adelaide Arcade and the historic Adelaide Gaol to the contemporary wonder of the SAHMRI complex.

Exploring Adelaide's legacy is like taking a trip back in time, as you embrace the stories inscribed in its streets, monuments, and galleries. Adelaide's heritage sites promise an enriching experience whether you're a history buff, an art enthusiast, or simply someone who enjoys the beauty of the past.

Chapter 3

NATURAL WONDERS AND OUTDOOR ADVENTURES

I'm overjoyed to discuss about Adelaide's natural treasures! Allow me to guide you through the stunning scenery and adventures that await you in this section of South Australia.

National Parks and Wildlife Reserves

Adelaide is endowed with breathtaking national parks and reserves. A few hours' drive from the city, the magnificent Flinders Ranges National Park features Rocky Mountains, historic canyons, and indigenous rock art. Cleland Conservation Park, located closer to Adelaide, provides a unique opportunity to engage with native Australian species.

Beach and Coastal Activities

The beaches, oh the beaches! Adelaide is surrounded by beautiful coasts that entice sunbathers and adventurers alike. There's a length of sand for everyone, from the bustling Glenelg Beach to the quiet shores of Semaphore. These beaches have it all: surfing, swimming, and sunbathing.

Nature Exploration and Hiking Trails

All nature lovers, unite! Adelaide has a network of beautiful paths for hikers of all skill levels. The Waterfall Gully to Mount Lofty Summit trek provides breathtaking views of the city, while Morialta Conservation Park is a waterfall chaser's paradise. Exploring the beautiful beauty of Belair National Park or the Botanic Gardens is an incredible treat.

Wildlife Encounters and Wildlife Refuges

Now, let's talk about wildlife! Adelaide has numerous amazing sanctuaries and conservation parks. Cleland Wildlife Park allows visitors to get up close and personal with classic Australian species such as kangaroos, koalas, and emus. With its expansive plains and large areas, Monarto Safari Park provides a one-of-a-kind safari experience where you may see African and local Australian species.

In Adelaide, nature truly steals the stage. There's an adventure waiting for you around every turn, whether you're drawn to the harsh terrains of national parks, the relaxing embrace of beaches, the energizing hikes, or the charm of native species. Prepare to be enthralled by the splendor of Adelaide's natural beauties.

Chapter 4

GASTRONOMY AND LOCAL CUISINE

Adelaide's culinary culture is a magnificent mash-up of history, creativity, and international flare. Let's dive into this culinary wonderland.

Adelaide Dishes

Adelaide has a superb choice of traditional cuisine when it comes to local pleasures. Taste the classic pie floater—a pork pie swimming in a pool of steaming hot pea soup—and embrace Aussie culture. The South Australian King Prawn is a local delicacy for seafood enthusiasts. And, of course, don't leave without trying one of Balfours' famed custard-filled pastries!

Culinary Experiences and Dining Options

Adelaide is a food lover's paradise! There's something for everyone's taste, from sophisticated restaurants to casual bistros. Rundle Street in the East End is a hive of activity, with cafes, bars, and fine-dining restaurants. Visit the Adelaide Central Market for a one-of-a-kind experience, where you can sample exquisite cheeses, gourmet chocolates, and fresh fruit while interacting with local sellers.

Culinary Events and Markets

When it comes to markets, Adelaide has a wealth of culinary events and marketplaces that foodies appreciate. The Adelaide Showground Farmers Market is a veritable treasure trove of organic vegetables, handcrafted items, and delightful delights. Don't miss the Tasting Australia festival, an annual food and wine extravaganza that highlights the finest of South Australia's culinary offerings.

Fusion Dining and International Cuisine

Adelaide's eating scene is as varied as it gets. Enjoy fusion food that combines regional flavors with international influences. Shobosho serves contemporary Japanese meals, while Africola offers vivid African-inspired flavors. The city also has a diverse range of different cuisines, ranging from traditional Italian trattorias to fiery Thai street food.

Adelaide's gastronomic journey is a joy, rich with delicacies that represent the city's broad ethnic background. Every bite in Adelaide reveals a narrative of culinary quality and innovation, whether you're savoring local favorites, visiting bustling markets, or indulging in fusion cuisine. Prepare to have your taste buds tantalized and discover Adelaide's unique gastronomic tapestry.

Chapter 5

SHOPPING AND ARTISAN CRAFTS

Adelaide's shopping delights! Whether you're looking for one-of-a-kind crafts or the latest fashion trends, this city has something for everyone.

Artisan Crafts and Local Boutiques

Adelaide is home to a plethora of lovely boutiques and galleries selling one-of-a-kind handmade products and artisanal crafts. Explore small businesses offering anything from handmade apparel to handcrafted jewelry on Ebenezer Place in the East End. Don't miss Jam Factory, a creative hotspot that features amazing glassware, pottery, and modern art by local artists.

Souvenirs and traditional handicrafts

Look no farther if you're looking for mementos that capture the soul of Adelaide. The Adelaide Hahndorf Market is a wonderful trove of traditional handcrafted goods, including wooden toys, leather goods, and indigenous art, all of which make excellent souvenirs of your stay. The Central Market is also a great place to pick up gourmet foods and locally produced goods.

Markets and Shopping Centers

The markets in Adelaide are a dynamic reflection of the city's culture and way of life. Wander around Adelaide Central Market, a buzzing hub of activity where you can take in the sights, scents, and flavors of fresh produce, specialty delicacies, and handcrafted products. On Saturdays, the Gilles Street Market is a mecca for vintage clothing and one-of-a-kind discoveries.

Modern shopping malls and specialty stores

Adelaide has sophisticated malls and specialist businesses catering to a wide range of tastes for a dose of modern shopping. Rundle Mall is a well-known retail destination that houses both international and local designers. If you want high-end clothes, King William Road in Hyde Park is a stylish shopping destination with boutique fashion companies and luxury boutiques.

Adelaide's shopping culture is a delightful mix of modern and traditional, with something for everyone. Shopping here is about experiencing the city's rich culture and creativity, not just obtaining products. From charming boutiques highlighting local skills to lively markets packed with unique items. Adelaide's shopping precincts guarantee enriching and rewarding retail therapy, whether you're looking for a handcrafted keepsake or the latest current trends.

Chapter 6

RELAXATION AND WELLNESS

I'm very excited to explore the realm of leisure and wellness in Adelaide! This city not only captivates with its metropolitan bustle, but it also provides tranquil getaways and dynamic entertainment.

Spas and Wellness Facilities

Adelaide's wellness scene is a haven for relaxation. Pamper yourself at award-winning spas like The Mayfair, where you can rejuvenate with luxury treatments in opulent settings. Head to wellness centers that specialize in yoga, meditation, and alternative therapies for a comprehensive experience that creates perfect harmony between body and mind.

Natural Serenity Retreats

Adelaide's surrounds are a nature lover's paradise. The Adelaide Hills provide a tranquil retreat with stunning vistas and lovely villages. Mount Lofty Botanic Garden is a hidden treasure, offering a calm location with beautiful vistas. Another refuge is the Adelaide Zoo, which combines wildlife interactions with magnificent botanical settings.

Parks and Recreational Facilities

Adelaide is endowed with beautiful green places. The Adelaide Botanic Garden is a horticultural paradise with a broad assortment of flora to explore. The picturesque trails of the River Torrens Linear Park allow leisurely strolls or cycling. Don't miss the Adelaide Park Lands, a sprawling network of greenery and recreational areas strewn around the city.

Nightlife and entertainment

The nightlife in Adelaide is a rich tapestry of experiences. The East End is a magnet for entertainment, with a profusion of clubs, live music venues, and cocktail lounges. Rundle Street comes alive after dark, with a variety of food establishments, live performances, and pubs. The Adelaide Festival Centre provides world-class acts, enriching the city's nightlife with cultural diversity.

Adelaide strikes a balance between relaxation and excitement, with everything from peaceful wellness centers to a thriving nightlife. It's a city that encourages you to relax among the splendor of nature or to partake in its dynamic entertainment scene. Adelaide welcomes you with open arms, whether you want quiet in a spa, a serene escape in nature, or an evening of exciting entertainment.

Chapter 7

FAMILY-FRIENDLY ACTIVITIES

Adelaide's beautiful world of family-friendly activities! There's something genuinely unique about visiting this city with loved ones, especially with so many opportunities for people of all ages.

Children's and Family Activities

Adelaide is a family adventurer's dream. Visit the Adelaide Zoo, where children may see exotic creatures and learn about wildlife protection. The South Australian Museum is a treasure mine of history and natural wonders that make learning fun for both youngsters and adults.

Parks and Zoos for Families

Adelaide has beautiful parks that are ideal for family picnics and leisurely hikes. The Adelaide Botanic Garden, which includes the iconic Bicentennial Conservatory and the International Rose Garden, provides an engaging setting for youngsters to discover various plant species. Adelaide Himeji Garden, a peaceful Japanese garden, allowing families to unwind and enjoy the environment.

Kids Educational Outings

Make learning enjoyable by organizing educational tours throughout the city. For young space aficionados, the Adelaide Planetarium is a wonderful alternative. The Adelaide Central Market is an educational experience in and of itself—a bustling marketplace where children can find fresh vegetables, sample various foods, and learn about different cultures.

Recreational Facilities and Playgrounds

Adelaide is proud of its playgrounds and leisure facilities. Children may explore walking trails and witness native species at Morialta Conservation Park. Wigley Reserve and Semaphore Foreshore Park are great for family trips since they have playgrounds, picnic spots, and beautiful beach views.

Adelaide is an ideal destination for families looking for both fun and education. This city promises a lovely blend of learning and pleasure for children and adults alike, with engaging museums and interactive outdoor spaces. Adelaide invites families to make amazing experiences together by providing a variety of family-friendly activities.

Chapter 8

DAY TRIPS AND NEARBY ATTRACTIONS

Certainly! Exploring beyond of Adelaide's bounds opens up a world of various experiences, each with its own distinct appeal. Here are a few ideas for exciting day trips and neighboring attractions:

Visits to Surrounding Areas

Leaving Adelaide takes you to incredible places. A visit to the Barossa Valley is a must for wine connoisseurs. The beautiful vineyards and cellar doors offer a diverse cultural experience, with visitors able to sample world-class wines and gastronomic pleasures.

Visiting Surrounding Towns and Landmarks

A picturesque journey from Adelaide, the Fleurieu Peninsula has a plethora of activities. Victor Harbor is a charming coastal village ideal for a day excursion. Discover breathtaking coastlines, visit Granite Island, or take a horse-drawn tram across the causeway for an unforgettable adventure.

Natural Wonders and Scenic Drives

Taking picturesque drives around Adelaide is a treat. A short drive away are the Adelaide Hills, which promise beautiful vistas, attractive settlements like Hahndorf, and picturesque views from Mount Lofty Summit.

Historical and cultural excursions

Visit Port Adelaide, a historic precinct that showcases maritime heritage and lively street art. At the Adelaide Gaol, guided tours explore stories of convict history and life behind bars.

Day tours from Adelaide are a treasure mine of various experiences that are easily accessible. Whether touring wine districts, coastal villages, or natural wonders, Adelaide's experiences provide infinite discovery and unforgettable memories.

Chapter 9

ACCOMMODATIONS AND LODGING

Absolutely! Adelaide has a wide range of accommodation alternatives to suit a variety of tastes, offering a comfortable stay for every visitor. Allow me to walk you through the various hotel options available.

Resorts and Hotels

Adelaide has a diverse choice of hotels and resorts, from boutique hotels to opulent retreats. Elegant hotels line North Terrace in the center of the city, affording panoramic views of the River Torrens and the Adelaide Oval. These locations are ideal for guests looking for modern amenities and close access to key sites, making exploration easy.

Bed and Breakfasts and Guesthouses

Guesthouses and bed and breakfasts sprinkled throughout Adelaide's lovely districts are suitable for visitors seeking a more intimate and domestic experience. These motels frequently offer individualized service as well as a look into local lifestyles. From ancient homes converted into quaint lodgings to garden getaways, these locations provide a soothing environment away from the rush and bustle.

Inns and Vacation Rentals

Vacation rentals and inns are common, particularly in beachfront communities such as Glenelg. These alternatives are ideal for families or larger groups looking for a more spacious and self-contained stay. Enjoy the convenience of fully furnished apartments, beachfront homes, or quiet cottages, all of which provide a truly home-away-from-home experience.

Campgrounds and Recreational Vehicle Parks (RV Parks)

Nature lovers and outdoor enthusiasts will like the camping and RV parks in and around Adelaide. These locations, which are near national parks or along picturesque coasts, provide opportunities to connect with nature. Enjoy starry nights, picturesque treks, and group campfires to encourage traveler companionship.

Adelaide's lodging diversity guarantees that every traveler finds their ideal match, whether it's the convenience of a downtown hotel, the charm of a cozy bed and breakfast, the independence of a vacation rental, or the peace and quiet of a camping site. Adelaide hotel forms a vital part of the overall enjoyable experience of visiting this bustling city, with alternatives appealing to a variety of budgets and preferences.

Chapter 10

PRACTICAL INFORMATION

Let's get into the specifics of traveling in Adelaide.

Adelaide Transportation Options

Adelaide boasts an efficient and accessible public transit system that makes it easy to explore the city and its surrounding areas. The Adelaide Metro, which consists of buses, trains, and trams, has vast lines. The tramline, in particular, gives convenient access to significant downtown locations such as Glenelg Beach, Adelaide Oval, and the Adelaide Central Market. For guests looking for convenience, acquiring a MetroCard allows for seamless travel across these means of transportation while also offering lower costs.

Local Transportation and Rental Services

Aside from public transportation, automobile rentals and ride-sharing services allow visitors to explore Adelaide at their own time. Rental businesses provide a wide selection of automobiles, ranging from compact cars for city exploration to larger vehicles for day trips to local wineries or national parks. Within the city, ride-sharing services such as Uber and Ola operate, giving an alternate means of transportation, particularly for shorter distances.

Contact Information and Emergency Services

It is critical to have access to important contacts and emergency services while traveling. In Australia, the emergency hotline numbers for police, fire, and medical aid are all the same. It's also a good idea to know the local phone numbers for tourist information centers, your country's embassy or consulate, and the front desk of your hotel. These contacts can be of critical assistance in the event of an emergency or an unforeseen incident.

Traveling in a Responsible Manner

Responsible travel is an essential part of experiencing any destination. Respect for local cultures and the environment is highly appreciated in Adelaide. As a tourist, it is critical to be cautious of trash and to keep public spaces clean. Using reusable water bottles and avoiding plastic waste are examples of eco-friendly actions that match with Adelaide's commitment to sustainability.

Adelaide's efficient public transportation, supplemented by rental services and ride-sharing choices, ensures seamless mobility within and around the city. Knowing important emergency contacts and practicing appropriate travel habits enhances the whole experience and adds to a healthy relationship with the city and its residents.

Conclusion

DEPARTING ADELAIDE WITH CHERISHED MEMORIES

Departing Adelaide feels like saying goodbye to a dear friend, since this city leaves indelible memories. Adelaide, which welcomed me as a curious traveler at first, has now become a treasured chapter in my trip journals.

Adelaide's Attractiveness

My departure is difficult since I am leaving behind a city that seamlessly blends culture, legacy, and modern charm. The friendliness of its people, as well as the bustling streets pulsing with activity, will be with me long after I go. The city's stunning skyline, decorated with historic landmarks and modern constructions, will live on in my recollections for the rest of my life.

Remembering Adelaide's Heritage

Adelaide's historical allure is unmistakable. Its heritage sites, museums, and indigenous areas tell the story of a rich past. Exploring the landmark Adelaide Oval or the South Australian Museum revealed layers of history that made an unforgettable impression on my travel experiences. The architectural marvels of the city, from colonial-era structures to modern architectural wonders, spoke eloquently about its growth.

Taking Advantage of Adelaide's Natural Beauty

Nature in Adelaide is a magnificent symphony. The huge parks and reserves, notably the spectacular Adelaide Botanic Garden and Cleland Conservation Park, provided tranquil respites from the hustle and bustle of city life. Glenelg Beach's coastal grandeur and the captivating paths in the Adelaide Hills remain clear in my mind, serving as a reminder of Adelaide's natural majesty.

Adelaide's Culinary Highlights

Adelaide's food scene is a delectable mingling of tastes. From traditional Adelaide delicacies to international cuisines, each taste provided a peek into the city's cultural variety. The lively markets and culinary events were a celebration of community and shared experiences, not just food.

Adelaide's shopping and entertainment districts.

Exploring Adelaide's shopping districts and unique boutiques was a thrilling experience in and of itself. The traditional handicrafts and trinkets I collected will be treasured keepsakes for the rest of my life. Adelaide's entertainment and nightlife, which included live music, cultural shows, and bustling pubs, portrayed the city as a thriving hub for both locals and tourists.

Leaving with Gratitude and Excitement

As I say goodbye to Adelaide, my heart is overflowing with gratitude for the experiences, hospitality, and memories this city has bestowed upon me. My leaving is not the conclusion, but rather the beginning of a journey back to this extraordinary place. Adelaide's allure has left a lasting imprint on me, and I leave with bated breath, knowing that I'll be dragged back into its arms sooner rather than later.

Last Thoughts

Adelaide is more than a city; it's an experience weaved with varied cultural strands and natural treasures. Departing from this incredible location may signal the end of a stay, but it also signals the beginning of a desire to return. Adelaide has a particular place in my heart because of its unique blend of history, landscape, gastronomy, and genuine welcome. Until we meet again, Adelaide - a temporary goodbye, but not forever.

Appendix

ADDITIONAL RESOURCES AND TRAVEL TIPS FOR ADELAIDE, SOUTH AUSTRALIA

The Appendix is a treasure mine of extra information, a backstage ticket to secrets and tips that may have slipped through the cracks in the chapters. It's where the pearls of wisdom and the last puzzle pieces are kept. Let's go into the Adelaide travel archive to find these hidden treasures.

Local Phrases and Lingo

Adelaide has its own variety of slang and colloquialisms that lend flavor to talks. Understanding these odd expressions, ranging from "heaps good" to "chucking a sickie," may be quite the cultural immersion. Embrace the local vernacular; it's a wonderful way to interact with the locals.

Calendar of Seasonal Events

Adelaide is a city that loves to party, and its events calendar is packed with interesting festivals and happenings all year. These events, ranging from the boisterous Fringe Festival to the vivacious Adelaide Festival of Arts, paint the city with a variety of cultural hues. The annual calendar includes a rich tapestry of music, arts, gastronomy, and other events.

Services and Emergency Contacts

First and foremost, safety! When exploring a new city, having the local emergency numbers, including police, ambulance, and fire services, is critical. It's always best to be prepared, and writing down these numbers could be a lifeline in an emergency.

List of Recommended Readings

A handpicked reading selection will help you delve further into Adelaide's history, culture, and tales. There are fascinating novels that offer unique perspectives on the city's past, inhabitants, and evolution. Consider purchasing a book by a local author or a historical narrative to further your awareness of this fascinating place.

Insider Information and Local Etiquette

Knowing the tourist attractions is only one aspect of navigating Adelaide like a local. Understanding local customs, tipping procedures, and respectful behavior will help you make relationships and immerse yourself in the city's vibe. These insider suggestions from seasoned locals might be priceless.

Resources for Language and Translation

While English is the most commonly spoken language, knowing a few simple words in other languages can be useful. Adelaide's multiculturalism means encountering a variety of languages. A simple "hello" or "thank you" in the recipient's original language frequently gets a smile and establishes rapport.

Checklist for Traveling

It's a good idea to make a checklist before embarking on any adventure to ensure a pleasant travel. From packing essentials to document reminders, this checklist is a traveler's best friend, ensuring that no important items are overlooked.

Navigational Aids and Maps

Some may be familiar with Adelaide's layout, but for others, possessing a city map or navigation aids can be a game changer. Whether you're traveling by foot, public transportation, or rental car, having a map handy can help you find hidden gems off the usual road.

Local Tour Operator Contact Information

Having contact information for local tour providers can open doors to unique activities for individuals looking for guided tours or specialty encounters. These operators are your gateway to bespoke excursions, whether it's a wine tour in the Adelaide Hills or an immersive cultural event.

Goodbye, but Not Farewell

As I jot down these additional resources and helpful hints, I'm reminded that even though I'm leaving Adelaide physically, the memories and knowledge I've learned from this city will always be a part of my traveler's toolkit. The Appendix, the book's final chapter, is a gateway to future adventures and an ode to the path

Adelaide has weaved into my soul. Adelaide, till we meet again, thank you for being a wonderful part in my trip story.

RECOMMENDED READING FOR ADELAIDE, SOUTH AUSTRALIA ENTHUSIASTS

As a traveler who has explored the nooks and crannies of Adelaide, South Australia, I've realized that beyond its magnificent landscapes and vibrant culture, the city has a literary universe that perfectly complements its appeal. Here are some intriguing reads that will help you connect with Adelaide even more:

"Adelaide: A Literary City"

This book is a love letter to Adelaide, written by local authors who know the city within and out. It's a collection of articles, poetry, and stories that celebrate Adelaide's unique character, people, and spirit. I got a newfound sense of admiration for this city's essence as I flipped through its pages.

"Barossa Food: From Our Beautiful Valley"

This book is a must-have for foodies, especially those visiting the adjacent Barossa Valley. It not only explores the delicious dishes and beverages, but it also tells the stories behind them. The rich history of winemaking and gastronomic experiences in this region make it a compelling read for any foodie.

"Colonial Ambition: A Novel of Early Adelaide"

With this historical tale, you can travel back in time to the early days of Adelaide. It clearly depicts the city's colonial past, presenting its founding people and the difficulties they encountered. The story weaves the growth of Adelaide, depicting its ambitions, hardships, and successes.

"Walking Adelaide: A Guide to the City's Historic Architecture"

This guide is a veritable trove for architectural fans and anybody interested in the city's history as told via its structures. Exploring Adelaide's streets through the prism of its architectural past exposes a wealth of stories carved in the city's structures. The book reveals the city's history and architectural growth, making every trip through Adelaide a journey through time.

"The Secret Lives of Adelaide Women: A Book of Days"

This fascinating book dives into the lives of the women who helped build Adelaide's history. It sheds light on their responsibilities, hardships, and contributions to the city's fabric via engaging stories and experiences. It's an engrossing read that unearths the unseen stories of the great women who have inspired Adelaide.

"Adelaide Noir"

"Adelaide Noir" provides an alternative vision of the city for those who prefer their stories to have a darker edge. It's a collection of noir-inspired stories that dive into Adelaide's underbelly, revealing its secrets and shadows. This book provides a distinct perspective, showcasing the city's unknown features.

"Adelaide: Nature of a City"

The essence of Adelaide's natural beauty is captured in this photographic tour. It highlights the city's different landscapes, parks, and wildlife through magnificent photos and informed commentary. It's a visual representation of Adelaide's coexistence with nature.

"Adelaide Cemeteries: A Celebratory History"

This unique book on Adelaide's cemeteries investigates the city's silent storytellers. These locations, in addition to being burial cemeteries, include historical information about the city. The book wonderfully describes the lives and legacies of individuals who are buried there, providing a unique insight into Adelaide's history.

Final Thoughts

Each page will act as a portal to learning the layers of Adelaide's identity as you immerse yourself in these reads. These publications will enrich your experience and deepen your connection with this interesting city, from its history and culture to its gastronomic delights and untold stories.

Sample Itinerary

SAMPLE ITINERARY FOR DIFFERENT TRAVELERS IN ADELAIDE, SOUTH AUSTRALIA

You're in for a treat when planning an itinerary for Adelaide. This city has a unique blend of culture, history, and natural beauty that begs to be discovered. Here's a sample itinerary to give you a taste of Adelaide's many attractions.

Day 1: Learn about Adelaide's history and culture.

Morning: Begin the day in Adelaide Central Market. It's a thriving hub where the city's culture and gastronomic delights collide. The scents, local products, and vendor conversation create an energizing ambiance.

Mid-morning: After some market goodies, visit the Adelaide Botanic Garden. This tranquil oasis within the metropolis provides a welcome escape from the city's bustle. Stroll through the lush foliage, admire the variety of plant species, and don't miss the landmark Bicentennial Conservatory.

Lunch: In North Adelaide, enjoy a lunch full of local cuisine. There are numerous attractive restaurants serving anything from gourmet food to light nibbles.

Afternoon: Visit the South Australian Museum to learn about Adelaide's history. Explore Aboriginal culture, natural history, and engaging displays that tell the story of the city's past.

Evening: Finish the day at Adelaide Oval. Catch a cricket match if one is scheduled, or simply take a guided tour to learn about the historic venue's sporting history.

Day 2: Natural and Scenic Beauty

Morning: Get up early and travel to Adelaide Hills. Visit Mount Lofty Summit for spectacular views of the city. The fresh morning air and breathtaking scenery make for an excellent start to the day.

Afternoon: visit Hahndorf, Australia's oldest surviving German community. Take a walk down the main street, which is dotted with boutique boutiques, galleries, and cafes. Remember to sample some apple strudel!

Lunch: Have lunch at one of Adelaide Hills' gorgeous wineries. In the midst of stunning vineyard vistas, savor local wines combined with delectable regional cuisine.

Afternoon: Visit Cleland fauna Park, a sanctuary for native Australian fauna. Get up close and personal with kangaroos, koalas, and other famous Australian animals.

Evening: Return to the city and unwind with a stroll along Glenelg Beach's promenade. Enjoy the sunset over the water while eating dinner at one of the seaside eateries.

Day 3: City Vibes and Contemporary Delights

Morning: Visit the Art Gallery of South Australia in the morning, which has an excellent collection of Australian and foreign art. Explore the galleries, which are filled with amazing artworks and thought-provoking exhibitions.

Mid-morning: Take a stroll down North Terrace. It is the location of the State Library, Parliament House, and other historical structures, each having its own narrative to tell.

Lunch: Indulge in a superb meal at one of the city's trendy cafés or eateries. There are numerous options available to suit every taste.

Afternoon: Take a stroll through Rundle Mall, Adelaide's top retail destination. There's a lot to discover, from high-end boutiques to offbeat stores and street performers.

Evening: Round out your Adelaide experience with a performance at the Adelaide Festival Centre. Attend a performance, whether theater, dance, or music, and become immersed in the city's cultural environment.

Final Thoughts

This schedule only touches the surface of what Adelaide has to offer. Adelaide has something for everyone, from its rich history and diverse culture to its spectacular natural landscapes and urban delights. Explore, roam, and let the city enchant you around every corner.

Printed in Great Britain
by Amazon

43229941R00030